NICK F

CW00822429

Touching
Down

Prayers for daily life

**kevin
mayhew**

First published in 2005 by

KEVIN MAYHEW LTD
Buxhall, Stowmarket, Suffolk, IP14 3BW
E-mail: info@kevinmayhewltd.com
www.kevinmayhew.com

9 8 7 6 5 4 3 2 1 0

ISBN 1 84417 498 0
Catalogue No. 1500864

Cover design by Angela Selfe
Edited and typeset by Katherine Laidler

Printed and bound in Great Britain

Contents

To my dear sister Ness –
valued more than you know

Introduction

There's an old saying you'll no doubt have heard, suggesting that we can sometimes be too heavenly minded to be of any earthly use. When it comes to prayer that's an undeniable danger, for we tend to assume we should focus on spiritual or religious things; predominantly, in other words, on God and the things of his kingdom. To a point, of course, that's entirely right, but to approach prayer solely from that perspective runs the risk of putting the cart before the horse, because, for me at least, prayer is often most meaningful when it arises directly from daily life. If we can only learn to see it, even the most ordinary moments can speak powerfully of God's presence, everyday objects and experiences able to point to deeper realities that inspire prayer and yield an encounter with the divine.

In this book, as in the companion volumes *Touched by His Hand* and *Heaven Touching Earth*, I attempt to approach prayer from that down-to-earth perspective, relating it to the commonplace, and thus breaking down the divide between sacred and secular, spiritual and worldly. Stripped of religious jargon as far as possible, here are prayers rooted in everyday life – the mundane providing a backdrop to a living encounter with God. Things as ordinary as a tap, feather duster, shopping trolley or even a burst pipe, point beyond themselves, providing a launch pad for further reflection.

The writer G. K. Chesterton once said, 'Only a fool tries to get the heavens into his head; the wise man is quite content to get his head into the heavens.' It is my hope that this book will help make possible the latter, helping you to glimpse God in such a way that your faith touches down to earth and your life in turn is touched by heaven. Achieve that, and instead of prayer being some rarefied activity, it will be as natural as breathing, every moment, no matter how routine, made special through knowing that God is a part of it.

NICK FAWCETT

1

The sea wall

It had taken a pounding,
   day after day,
   year after year,
   the mighty sea relentlessly renewing its attack
   as wave after wave hurled itself against the wall
   and exploded in a cloud of spray.
Yet still it stood,
   solid and defiant,
   a massive bulwark guarding the town beyond.

Thank you, Lord, for guarding me,
   faithfully providing shelter and protection
   when storms brew
   and waves threaten to sweep me away.
Thank you for the strength of your love
   and certainty of your promise,
   the knowledge that though all else may pass away
   your goodness will continue,
   solid and secure in an ever-changing universe.
Whatever I face, I will not fear,
   for you are with me,
   the same yesterday, today and for ever.
Amen.

2
The moth

It fluttered around the flame,
    inexorably drawn –
    surely sensing the danger
    yet unable to resist –
    and it was only a matter of time
    before its wings were scorched
    and the hapless creature fell.

Like the moth, Lord, I am attracted by what destroys,
    promising life yet delivering death.
I try to fight it,
    aware of the danger,
    but the lure is too strong,
    all sense forgotten when temptation strikes.
Draw me close to you,
    and shine in my darkness,
    bringing the light that leads to life.
Amen.

3
The bookmark

It marked my place in the book,
    showing how much I'd read
    and how much was left,
    saving me from the chore, after putting it aside,
    of thumbing through the pages
    to find the point I'd reached.

Though there's no such simple tool, Lord,
    in the unfolding story of faith,
    help me to gauge my progress there,
    recognising how far I've come
    and how far I've yet to go.
Save me from going back over the same old ground
    and settling for the familiar and undemanding,
    but save me also from getting ahead of myself,
    believing that the tale is complete
    when it's barely started.
Show me where I am
    and where you would have me be,
    and, as I continue the saga of discipleship,
    help me to advance, page by page,
    to a deeper knowledge of you.
Amen.

4
The JCB

It moved into action,
    flexing its mechanical muscles,
    and the walls tumbled before it,
    bricks and mortar falling like confetti,
    nothing able to obstruct its relentless progress
    as it reduced the building to a pile of rubble –
    what had taken months to build
    destroyed in a few moments.

It's easy to tear down, Lord –
    I do it all the time.
Through a harsh word or critical look,
    I rip the ground from beneath people's feet,
    undermining their confidence
    and demolishing their self-esteem.
Forgive me for finding fault,
    magnifying weaknesses and dwelling on mistakes,
    and instead of putting people down,
    help me to build them up –
    constructive in all I do, think and say.
Amen.

5
The handwriting

It was barely legible,
    an indecipherable scrawl,
    yet to the trained eye it was far more,
    every dot, squiggle, line and curve
    saying as much as the words,
    if not more,
    revealing the quirks, traits, strengths and weaknesses
    of the one who wrote it.

Teach me, Lord, to glimpse you in the daily round of life
    and the wonder of this world.
Where others look and see nothing,
    help me to observe with the eye of faith,
    perceiving the reality beneath the surface.
Open my heart as well as my eyes,
    that I may look and truly see.
Amen.

6
The birthday card

It was greeted with excitement,
    hastily torn open in anticipation of a gift inside –
    yet another birthday surprise.

It was greeted with pride,
    for it represented a coming of age,
    a personal milestone,
    the start of a new and exciting chapter.

It was greeted with resignation,
    for it meant another year gone by,
    another year older –
    too much of life gone,
    too little yet to come.

Whatever my stage of life, Lord,
    help me to greet it thankfully,
    knowing that as you have blessed me
    so you will bless me again –
    each moment given by you,
    and with the best yet to come.
Amen.

7
The Olympic torch

They all played a part,
    each athlete carrying the torch a stage along the way,
    the job not just a duty but a joy,
    a privilege held on trust,
    for they were proud to bear it, if only for a moment,
    and to pass it on to others.

Teach me, Lord, to hold aloft the torch of faith,
    bearing it with equal pride and fervour.
Help me to do my bit,
    through word and deed faithfully handing it on,
    so that others might receive and pass it on in turn:
    a flame of love,
    symbol of hope
    and beacon of truth –
    light for all the world.
Amen.

8
The rulebook

It was a daunting list,
    a rule, it seemed, for every occasion –
    how to do this,
    how not to do that –
    and woe betide any who got things wrong.

I still see *you* like that, Lord,
    though I know I shouldn't;
    still perceive you as a setter of rules:
    he who must be obeyed.
Teach me
    that you are not always looking over my shoulder,
    waiting to trip me up,
    but that you stand by my side,
    always ready to affirm and encourage,
    inviting me to share your life
    and be truly free.
Amen.

9

The personalised number plate

It was more than a number,
   almost a name,
   chosen for a reason
   and secured at some cost,
   this number plate,
   unlike others,
   saying more about the driver than the car,
   the person than the machine.

Teach me, Lord, that *I'm* more than a number to you,
   more even than just a name;
   that you value me as an individual,
   for who and what I am
   and all that I can be.
Remind me that I too am unique in your eyes,
   chosen and precious to you,
   and that you willingly paid the ultimate price
   so that I might know you in person
   as you know me.
Amen.

10
The Botox injection

'No more wrinkles,' it said.
'Roll back the years!'
And there was no denying she looked good,
   her skin smoother and firmer than it had been before.
But did she *feel* different, that was the question,
   not just more confident in her appearance
   but fitter,
   younger,
   energised within?
She could change the outside,
   but what of the rest:
   the attitudes and ideas that shaped her life,
   making her the person she was?

Lord, I don't like growing older
   any more than the next person,
   but though I can disguise the signs of ageing
   I can never deny them,
   for they are more than skin deep.
Teach me, as *you* do, to accept who I am,
   and to place into your hands everything I yet might be,
   recognising that you alone
   are able to bring true renewal,
   not just now
   but for evermore.
Amen.

11
The armchair

It was comfortable –
   too comfortable –
   enticing me simply to lie back,
   relax
   and let the world go by.
Nothing wrong with that, of course,
   for work without rest is no good to anyone,
   but I also need exercise and activity,
   these equally vital if I hope to stay in shape.

Forgive, Lord, my laziness in discipleship,
   my inclination to lounge in the comfort zone
   rather than stretch the muscles of faith.
Forgive me for reducing what ought to be a way of life
   to a casual pursuit,
   a couch potato commitment that asks little
   and delivers less.
Teach me to work at my faith,
   so that it not only shapes every aspect of life
   but is kept in shape in turn.
Amen.

12

The sewage works

It's not a pretty sight
   nor a pretty subject,
   but it's invaluable nonetheless,
   for without it we'd be overwhelmed
   by waste and disease,
   our world contaminated beyond our worst nightmares,
   fit for nothing and no one.

Too much, Lord, contaminates my life –
   impure thoughts,
   foolish words
   and thoughtless actions;
   a host of attitudes, desires, weaknesses and faults
   that pollute and destroy.
And, hard though I try,
   I cannot rid myself of them,
   their hold on me too great.
Reach out in mercy,
   and cleanse me of all that undermines my inner health,
   so that, by your love, I may be truly whole.
Amen.

13

The recycling centre

It was a heartwarming sight,
    all kinds of items recycled for further use –
    clothes, plastic, paper, glass
    and so much else that had been thrown away –
    humbling but sobering to see so much saved
    that would otherwise have been lost for ever.

We've made progress, Lord,
    but not much,
    each of us still part of a disposable culture,
    a society that consumes resources
    with little thought of tomorrow
    and still less for others.
Give me a greater sense of responsibility
    to future generations
    and to you;
    an appreciation of the countless blessings
    I have received
    and the duty I have to use them wisely,
    so that others may enjoy them in turn.
Amen.

14
The burst pipe

It didn't look much,
    just a small hole in the pipe,
    but water gushed from it –
    through the ceiling,
    down the walls
    and across the floor –
    leaving the room sodden,
    décor ruined.

Lord, my faults seem small,
    barely worth bothering with sometimes,
    yet the consequences can be greater than I expect,
    an apparently trivial mistake
    having potentially devastating repercussions.
However minor my weaknesses may be,
    teach me to consider where they might lead
    and to put things right
    before lasting damage is done.
Amen.

15
The tunnel

It was an eerie experience,
    the darkness becoming ever deeper
    until it enveloped me completely,
    leaving me blundering about in confusion,
    all sense of direction lost.
But then a chink of light,
    distant but unmistakable,
    and I pressed on towards it,
    emerging finally into the brightness of day
    and the warmth of the sun.

Support me, Lord, when my mood is black,
    life seeming dark beyond redemption.
Though I feel hopelessly lost –
    unsure where to turn next,
    unsure of everything –
    teach me that there is always light
    at the end of the tunnel
    and that your love will guide me to it.
Amen.

16

The book review

I read the review,
   happy with it,
   and a touch smug
   for it concerned *my* book,
   my work,
   and the comments were good,
   supportive throughout.
I read another . . .
   and my face fell,
   for it was the same book
   but a different response –
   positives certainly,
   but negatives too.
Yet I learned from both,
   as much from the second as the first,
   perhaps even more from the second.

Teach me, Lord, to listen not just to those who praise me
   but to those who see my faults;
   to remember that an honest critic
   can be my truest friend,
   pointing not simply to what I *like* to hear
   but what I *need* to hear
   if I would truly grow.
Amen.

17

The seeds

He sowed the seeds,
   then wished he hadn't,
   for the plants took over,
   vigorous to a fault,
   and, once established, they were hard to shift,
   seeming to have a mind of their own,
   intent on survival.

Remind me, Lord, that in all kinds of ways
   I reap what I sow,
   for better or for worse,
   words and deeds long buried bursting into life,
   bringing joy or sorrow,
   satisfaction or shame.
Before I speak or act, then,
   teach me to pause and ponder,
   lest in sowing the seed
   I reap the whirlwind.
Amen.

18
The mountain spring

It bubbled up,
   sparkling and irrepressible,
   gurgling with delight as it cascaded down the hillside;
   and I stooped to drink,
   marvelling at its taste,
   the water cool and clear,
   never running dry.

Your love, Lord, wells up the same,
   day upon day,
   year upon year,
   an unfailing spring of living water,
   poured out beyond my deserving
   so that my cup overflows.
For your faithful blessing,
   so freely given,
   so joyfully received,
   receive my praise.
Amen.

19
The graffiti

The wall was covered,
    obliterated by a hotchpotch of words and pictures,
    some smutty,
    others obscene,
    a few touched by humour,
    most driven by hate,
    yet all springing from a common desire
    to leave some mark;
    to shout defiantly to the world:
    'I was here!'

What mark will *I* leave, Lord, when my course is run?
What imprint will I have made,
    not on bricks and mortar
    but on human hearts?
Help me to live in such a way
    that my words and deeds speak of you,
    testament not to my brief span but to your eternal love,
    and may that be legacy enough.
Amen.

20
The can of Pepsi

Thirst-quenching, they called it,
   and I suppose it was in its way,
   but whether it measured up
   to more extravagant claims –
   lip-smackin', ace-tastin', motivatin',
   good-buzzin', cool-talkin', high-walkin',
   fast-livin', ever-givin', cool-fizzin' –
   I somehow doubt.

I thirst for many things in life, Lord,
   some more than others –
   luxury, riches and success among them –
   but few live up to expectations,
   still less fully satisfy.
Teach me to drink of living water,
   the new wine you offer in Christ,
   and never to thirst again.
Amen.

21
The operating theatre

They didn't give much for his chances,
    for the operation was a major one,
    involving complex and dangerous surgery.
Yet he not only pulled through
    but was a changed man afterwards,
    enjoying a quality of life undreamt of before.

Examine me, Lord, and make me whole.
Put a new heart and right spirit within me,
    and restore me in body, mind and spirit.
Come now
    and transform my life
    by your healing, redeeming touch.
Amen.

22

The wrestlers

They played their part well,
    the two of them seemingly locked in combat,
    straining every sinew to secure a hold or a lift,
    but for much of the time
    they were merely playing to the gallery,
    the action stage-managed,
    a carefully contrived charade.

I struggle, Lord, every day,
    not with flesh and blood but faith and doubt,
    wanting to serve you yet beset by temptation,
    attempting to trust yet plagued by fears,
    striving to believe yet perplexed by questions,
    resolved to be strong yet proving weak.
Teach me truly to wrestle with such things –
    not going through the motions
    but giving my all,
    confident that though I am weak,
    you are strong,
    and victory is assured.
Amen.

23

The teenager

A difficult age, they called it,
    and so it was,
    not just for his parents but for him as well:
    a time for finding his feet
    and developing his own identity,
    and inevitably that involved rebellion at times,
    reacting against received wisdom
    and challenging the status quo
    until he'd worked out for himself
    where he stood and why.

Teach me, Lord,
    that rebellion has a place in *discipleship* too:
    that genuine commitment
    sometimes means questioning the ways of the world
    and being ready, where necessary,
    to protest against accepted norms,
    confronting wrongs and combating evil,
    however unpopular that may make me.
Though I mellow with the years,
    keep alive the defiance of youth
    when it comes to standing up for you.
Amen.

24
The curtains

The sun was too bright,
   pouring in through the window,
   so I pulled across the curtains
   until the light dimmed
   and I could open them once more.
But when it grew dark,
   I closed them again,
   this time keeping light *in* lest prying eyes intrude.

Forgive me, Lord,
   for I do much the same with *your* light,
   stopping it from both shining in or out.
Pull back the curtains I close against you,
   so that the light of your love
   and radiance of your presence
   may flood into my heart
   and out through my life.
Amen.

24
The kookaburra

It wasn't real laughter,
    just the strident call of a kookaburra
    but it sounded full of fun;
    and all who heard it walked off with a chuckle,
    the sound infectious,
    impossible to resist.

Help me, Lord, to spread a little happiness,
    contagious joy bubbling up within me.
Teach me to live with a smile in my heart
    and laughter on my lips,
    each day celebrating your love
    in a way that invites others to share it in turn.
Amen.

26

The tossed coin

'Heads,' I called,
    and heads it was,
    the business resolved on the toss of a coin.
Not the best way, perhaps, to settle an issue,
    not an important one, anyway,
    but in this case it did the job –
    a simple matter
    simply resolved.

I wish all choices were that easy, Lord,
    as swift and straightforward to deal with,
    but they're not,
    most being far more complex –
    what seems right to some seeming wrong to others.
Give me wisdom, then, in all my decisions,
    and, above all, the courage I need
    both to make them
    and to amend them when I get them wrong.
Amen.

27
The overheated radiator

It was bound to happen,
    the sun hot and traffic at a standstill,
    but that wasn't the root of the problem,
    the reason he stood there now,
    steam billowing from the bonnet.
The radiator leaked,
    and he knew it,
    but he'd failed to have it fixed,
    failed even to replenish it that morning,
    and inevitably he'd paid the price.

Forgive me, Lord, for I too can overheat,
    and though there are many reasons,
    it's finally down to me,
    my neglect of you and failure to grow in grace.
Fill me with gentleness, patience and self-control,
    so that should steam start to rise,
    you may channel it safely
    and help me to cool off,
    before *all* pay the price.
Amen.

28

The sports commentator

He was irritating at times,
    trotting out the predictable clichés and trivia,
    yet he nonetheless added immeasurably
    to my enjoyment,
    helping me not only to understand
    what was happening
    but also to appreciate the finer points,
    his words giving names to faces
    and bringing events to life.

In faith, Lord, as much as anything,
    I need help to get the picture,
    for there are gaps in my knowledge,
    details I find hard to grasp,
    not least in the study of your word.
Teach me to appreciate those who offer guidance –
    preachers,
    teachers,
    scholars,
    writers –
    all whose insights lead to deeper perception
    and a fuller experience of your love,
    and, in humility, may I listen and learn.
Amen.

29

The marathon runners

They assembled in their thousands,
    chatting and laughing companionably –
    all sorts,
    all shapes,
    all ages –
    some there to win,
    others to raise money,
    others simply to have fun,
    but all united,
    not just in their resolve to finish the course
    but in the camaraderie of taking part,
    the privilege of running the race together.

Teach me, Lord, in the marathon journey of faith,
    that I run not *against* others
    but *with* them,
    part of the great company of your people,
    sharing a common cause
    and seeking the same goal.
For the solidarity that brings,
    the support and encouragement
    both given and received,
    receive my thanks.
Amen.

30
The cockerel

It was an unfamiliar sound for a townsperson like me –
    a cock crowing at the crack of dawn –
    and for a moment I groaned in dismay,
    eyes still heavy with sleep.
But then a shaft of sunlight flooded the room
    and the sound of birdsong
    drifted through the window –
    reminders of another day,
    new beginnings –
    and I rose joyfully,
    thankful for its promise.

Teach me, Lord, to greet each day with gratitude,
    awakening with a sense of joy and expectation
    at the possibilities of life.
Whatever fears I may have or problems I may be facing,
    help me to welcome the new morning as your gift
    and to live every moment as fully as I am able.
Amen.

31
The dust

It lay everywhere –
    thick upon each surface,
    and in each nook and cranny of the house –
    a sombre reminder of the fate we share:
    our striving and dreams,
    our very self,
    destined to turn to dust.

Yet from the dust of the earth, Lord,
    you fashioned our bodies and gave us life.
And though to the ground we return –
    dust to dust,
    ashes to ashes –
    you promise us new beginnings:
    love that will neither fade nor perish,
    a kingdom that never ends.
Let us speak, then, not of death and decay,
    but of your new creation,
    life for evermore.
Amen.

32
The tap

I turn on the tap,
   and there it is,
   water when and where I want it –
   to wash the dishes,
   water the garden,
   take a bath,
   have a drink,
   and so much else besides –
   enough, and more than enough, for all my needs.

Forgive me, Lord,
   for I treat *you* like a tap sometimes,
   expecting you to supply whatever I want,
   whenever I want it –
   blessings on demand.
Remind me that you *do* provide –
   more than I can ever ask for –
   but not necessarily the things of this world,
   your gifts of a different kind,
   nurturing the spirit and enriching within.
Teach me to thirst for such things –
   gifts of your kingdom –
   and to be truly satisfied.
Amen.

33

The dinosaur bones

They were ancient,
    a reminder of life forms that walked the earth
    not just centuries but aeons ago –
    for millions of years masters of all they surveyed –
    the whole of human history, by comparison,
    just a tiny speck,
    a mere drop in the ocean.
Yet now they are gone,
    the only clue to their existence a few fossil remains,
    silent witness to a bygone age.

You alone, Lord, are eternal,
    the same yesterday, today and tomorrow.
You alone are before and beyond all,
    the beginning and end of everything that is,
    has been
    and shall be.
Yet you invite us,
    seemingly here today and gone tomorrow –
    like flowers fleetingly in bloom –
    to share in eternity,
    one with you for evermore.
For the breadth of your purpose
    and wonder of your grace,
    Lord, thank you.
Amen.

34
The collage

It couldn't have been more ordinary, in a sense,
   for it was made from everyday items –
   scraps and objects that are two a penny,
   barely noticed, let alone valued –
   yet together they made something extraordinary,
   a collage of startling beauty.

Take, Lord, the unpromising material of my life –
   the unremarkable gifts,
   commonplace weaknesses,
   everyday traits
   and average achievements –
   and fashion from it all a new person,
   something special for you.
Amen.

35

The bookmakers

They have it right most of the time,
  experience having taught them to weigh up the odds
  and adjust them as necessary,
  but,
  just occasionally,
  a rank outsider springs a surprise,
  coming through to take the prize.

Remind me, Lord, that you are a God of surprises,
  constantly overturning the expectations of this world,
  turning weakness to strength,
  despair to hope
  and defeat to victory.
Teach me, then,
  however much I feel up against it,
  however daunting the challenge
  and feeble my resources,
  to trust in you,
  knowing that nothing finally
  will be able to frustrate your will
  or deny the triumph of your love.
Amen.

36
The free gift

'Congratulations!' it said.
'You have won our bumper prize:
   the holiday of a lifetime,
   absolutely free,
   not to be missed.'
But it *wasn't* free,
   nowhere near it,
   for concealed in the small print,
   tucked neatly out of view,
   lay a host of hidden costs,
   the amount I'd eventually pay
   far greater than any 'gift' I'd receive.

Thank you, Lord, that *your* gifts are truly free:
   your love, mercy, joy and peace,
   blessings too many to number
   offered without strings attached.
Thank you for paying the price of these yourself,
   sharing our flesh,
   bearing our pain
   and dying our death,
   so that we might receive life,
   now and for all eternity,
   a prize indeed too special to miss.
Amen.

37
The parrot

It sounded good –
    an accomplished repertoire for a *person*,
    let alone a *parrot*!
Only, of course, I wasn't fooled,
    for though it seemed to speak,
    made all the right noises,
    it did so mechanically,
    simply repeating what it had heard,
    with no idea of the meaning,
    the sense behind the words.

Forgive me, Lord,
    for so much of my faith is parroted –
    imitation commitment,
    pastiche discipleship –
    sounding impressive,
    looking the part,
    yet in reality borrowed from others,
    echoing their experiences,
    using their language,
    repeating the established jargon,
    without truly speaking *to* and *for* me.
Draw me close to you each day
    in a deep and vibrant relationship,
    so that what I say with my lips
    I may truly believe in my heart.
Amen.

38
The reporter

She was there on the scene,
   swift to report the facts –
   to pass on, as best she could,
   everything she'd seen and heard –
   her story not simply gleaned from others
   and cobbled together
   but written on the spot:
   an eyewitness account as events unfolded.

Teach me, Lord, to witness authentically to you,
   speaking from personal experience
   of what I've found to be true.
Help me to bring to life the reality of your love,
   telling of the blessings you've given,
   guidance offered,
   mercy shown
   and peace imparted.
You have given me good news,
   glad tidings for all.
Help me to share it.
Amen.

39
The clowns

It was the usual slapstick stuff,
    predictable to say the least,
    but the kids loved it,
    roaring their approval,
    rolling about in glee.
They saw the *mask*, that's all,
    the painted smile,
    and why not? –
    there'd be time enough in later years
    to understand the tears.

Remind me, Lord, that what I see of others
    is rarely the whole story;
    that behind the façade,
    beneath the veneer,
    most of them wrestle with their secret pain,
    hidden fears
    and inner turmoil –
    casualties of the hurly-burly of life.
Teach me that beneath the public face
    there lies a private world,
    and help me in all my dealings to allow for both.
Amen.

40
The football scarf

He wore it with pride,
    happy to be associated with his team,
    their trials and disappointments,
    victories and defeats,
    the scarf being more than an item of clothing –
    a way rather of identifying himself with the players,
    displaying his allegiance to all.

Am I proud, Lord, to be linked with you,
    ready in turn to show where my loyalties lie?
Or am I a closet disciple,
    hiding my faith away
    for fear of what others might think,
    should they know where I truly stand?
Teach me never to be ashamed of you,
    lest the day come when I find you ashamed of me.
Amen.

41

The adult learning centre

They were a good age, some of them –
   fifty,
   sixty,
   even seventy –
   but they weren't afraid to admit
   the gaps in their knowledge,
   nor to do something about it,
   each more than ready to apply themselves to study:
   to listen and learn.

Forgive me, Lord,
   for I've become complacent,
   assuming I've grasped all I need to know,
   no longer a novice at discipleship but a graduate,
   my education complete.
Teach me that, for all my years of faith,
   there is more still to be learned,
   much that I've barely begun to explore.
Instruct me, then, in your ways,
   and lead me to ever-deeper understanding.
Amen.

42
The MOT

It wasn't welcome, to put it mildly,
    but it was necessary,
    the checks vital to ensure the car was safe,
    the brakes, lights, seatbelts and so forth
    all as they should be,
    fit for the road.

Am *I* ready, Lord,
    in shape for the journey ahead?
Are the mechanics of discipleship in place,
    the nuts and bolts of faith firmly secured?
I like to think so,
    but I rarely take time to check,
    assuming instead that everything will take care of itself.
Test me
    and correct my faults,
    examine me
    and tune my will to yours,
    so that, however demanding the road,
    I may travel it safely with you
    until the journey's end.
Amen.

43
The shadow

A shadow fell across us,
    and the world felt darker,
    the air suddenly cool,
    yet the sun was still shining,
    as bright and warm as ever,
    the shade cast *because* of its presence
    not despite it.

Remind me, Lord, that,
    in this life,
    there can be no sun without shadow
    or laughter without tears,
    and that sometimes the darkness seems deeper
    the more the light shines.
Teach me, then, however dark the shade,
    to keep faith,
    trusting that, despite appearances,
    you are there.
Amen.

44

The hearing aid

It changed her life,
    what had been indistinct suddenly clear,
    opening up again not just conversation
    but delight in the song of birds,
    the sound of music,
    the splash of waves
    and the laughter of children –
    a world of sense that had long been closed.

Help *me* to hear, Lord,
    not with my ears but with my heart –
    to hear your voice in those around me,
    your word in prayer and worship,
    your call in the daily routine,
    your speech in the miracle of life.
Remind me of the many ways you speak,
    and give me a receptive spirit
    to hear what you are saying.
Amen.

45

The kestrel

It hovered overhead,
    scanning the ground below for movement,
    eyes only for the task in hand,
    all else blotted out.
Though the wind gusted and rain fell,
    though children played and cars raced by,
    it hung there still,
    motionless,
    focused,
    immune to all distractions.

Give me, Lord, a similar focus on you,
    the ability to concentrate my thoughts in daily devotion
    and faithful discipleship,
    making you the centre of all I do and am,
    the hub of my life and goal of all my being.
Whatever temptations and pressures I face,
    may nothing distract me from knowing you better
    and responding in grateful, loving service.
Amen.

46
The famine

They were shocking pictures,
    indescribably awful –
    scenes of appalling suffering and abject misery
    that brought tears to the eyes and a lump to the throat,
    yet I was no longer truly shocked
    for I'd seen them before –
    different people,
    different emaciated bodies and haunted faces
    yet the same scenes –
    history repeating itself time and again.

We speak of making poverty history, Lord,
    and we *have* done that,
    but not in the way intended.
We've made it part of our world,
    an accepted norm,
    a fact of life . . . and death . . . for countless millions,
    and though it's not all our doing,
    much of it down to forces beyond our control,
    we're all still complicit in the crime,
    none of us able to absolve ourselves fully
    of responsibility.
Forgive the evil of our world,
    and our share within it,
    and give us all a common resolve to tackle poverty
    and *truly* consign it to history.
Amen.

47

The G8 summit

They carried the world's hopes on their shoulders,
    a heavy load to bear,
    for though their citizens clamoured for change –
    wrongs put right
    and justice done –
    they knew all too well that those same people
    would swiftly protest
    should change prove costly,
    meaning *real* change,
    not just for others
    but for them.

Lord, I know that if evils are to be tackled
    it needs the will of politicians,
    governments and leaders,
    and I pray that they'll do their bit.
I know it needs fairer trade and relief of debt
    coupled with generous, genuine aid,
    and I pray these will be achieved.
But save me from using all this to pass the buck
    as though the ills of this world are not also down to me.
As well as *calling* for change,
    help me to change in turn,
    ready to play *my* part
    before I ask others to play *theirs*.
Amen.

48
The CCTV cameras

It was a strange feeling,
  reassuring yet also eerie,
  for I was being watched,
  my every move surveyed,
  the all-seeing eye of the camera taking everything in
  and storing it all away.

You, Lord, watch over me,
  hour after hour,
  day after day,
  not to keep tabs on what I do
  but as a loving friend and faithful companion –
  there to help in times of need,
  protect in times of danger
  and comfort in times of hurt.
Thank you for the knowledge that,
  though *I* lose sight of *you*,
  still *you* look out for *me*.
Amen.

49
The ferry boat

There was no way of swimming across,
    the water too deep and current strong,
    but the boat was waiting,
    ready, come wind or rain,
    to ply its way across to the other side.

Ferry me, Lord, through the straits of life,
    for I cannot get through alone.
In calm or tempest,
    sunshine or rain,
    carry me safely over the waters
    until I reach the shore
    and set foot in your kingdom.
Amen.

50
The rhubarb

I tried to eat it,
  but it was all that I could do,
  the taste bitter,
  bringing tears to the eyes –
  a meal put to waste
  for want of a little sweetness.

I've seen not just food ruined, Lord, but lives also,
  bitterness destroying what might have been,
  curdling the milk of human kindness,
  souring relationships,
  turning rancid what once brought joy.
Whatever hurts or disappointments I face,
  help me to deal with them and move on,
  lest in making a meal of them,
  they end up making a meal of me.
Amen.

51
The ACAS meeting

It looked hopeless,
    the two sides implacably opposed
    but the arbiters brought them together,
    listening, prompting, calming and cajoling –
    a voice of reason when wills clashed,
    of restraint when tempers frayed,
    of reconciliation when relations collapsed
    until finally,
    after months of talks,
    accord was reached
    and harmony restored.

Teach me, Lord,
    wherever and whenever I can,
    to be a peacemaker,
    not poking my nose in where it's not wanted,
    but ready,
    when I find myself caught in the middle of discord,
    to serve as a go-between,
    mediating your love.
Give me, then, sensitivity to calm the waters,
    wisdom to break the deadlock
    and love to heal the wounds.
Amen.

52
The board of trustees

It was an honour,
  but an onerous one,
  the future of thousands
  dependent on their stewardship,
  for the resources they administered were held on trust,
  representing not just assets but people –
  their savings and investments,
  lives and livelihoods.

You've honoured *us*, Lord,
  each and every one,
  placing in our care not just land or money
  but the world itself,
  an asset beyond price.
Forgive my share in squandering its resources,
  living today with no thought of tomorrow.
Forgive my betrayal of your trust,
  living with little thought
  for present and future generations.
Teach me to live wisely,
  mindful of all your creation,
  and grant that others may do the same.
Amen.

53
The recorder player

It was hardly a pleasant sound,
   more of a shrill blast,
   the child having little control of the instrument
   and apparently even less musical sense,
   yet she was enjoying herself,
   letting loose with unbridled glee.

I want to make music for you, Lord,
   to live my life as an exuberant melody of praise,
   offered in gratitude for all you've done
   and everything you'll always mean to me.
It may sometimes be out of tune,
   more of a joyful noise than work of art,
   but receive it, I pray,
   together with what I am and all I long to be,
   for it comes from the heart,
   with love.
Amen.

54
The alien

It was inhuman,
   literally,
   a monstrous creature from another world,
   with no scruples, compassion or feeling,
   mutilating bodies and destroying lives
   without even a shred of compunction.
But, of course, it wasn't real –
   just a figment of the author's imagination:
   an extraterrestrial dreamt up in the mind
   and brought to life on the screen.

I saw *more* inhumanity,
   more suffering and slaughter,
   only this time it was all too real –
   pictures on the television and in the papers
   of unspeakable carnage,
   lives cruelly shattered with equal lack of compunction.
And it was no alien to blame,
   but ordinary people,
   fellow human beings
   who somehow saw murder as their mission,
   killing as their calling.

Heal, Lord, our broken world,
   and put an end to its madness,
   so that, whatever divides,
   and whatever our colour, creed or culture,
   we may see beyond cause or grievance
   to the common humanity that unites us all.
Amen.

55

The cancer patient

The treatment was hard enough to bear –
   the hair loss, nausea and pain –
   and worse still was the fear,
   not just of suffering and slow decline
   but of being separated from loved ones;
   of finally saying goodbye.
Yet hardest of all were the awkward silences,
   forced smiles
   and well-meant platitudes –
   being seen not as a person but a patient,
   no longer an individual but a disease.

To all, Lord, wrestling with terminal illness,
   give the assurance that you will always value them
   for who they are;
   and help their families, friends and colleagues
   as they struggle to come to terms with their feelings,
   to do the same,
   seeing not the illness but the individual underneath.
Whatever else may be lost,
   may that continue,
   to the end
   and beyond.
Amen.

56
The toyshop

It was awash with delights . . .
    or at least it was for my children,
    their eyes round with wonder,
    fingers unable to resist picking up now this,
    now that –
    the range of toys and games so vast
    it was hard for them to choose.
And it would have been the same once for me,
    when I too would have felt similar excitement
    at such a sight.
Only, of course, childhood had passed,
    and I'd moved on,
    such pursuits long since left behind.

Have I moved on in *faith*, Lord,
    left former ways behind,
    or do I *play* at discipleship,
    treating it as a game
    instead of being serious about commitment?
Have I matured as a person,
    growing up not only as an individual
    but also in my dealings with others,
    or do I still lack maturity,
    being even infantile sometimes in my behaviour?
Teach me to be childlike in attitude
    but not childish,
    to display the trust, innocence and enthusiasm of youth,
    yet also the wisdom, sensitivity and understanding
    of later years.
Amen.

57

The hammer

I used a hammer to crack a nut . . .
   literally!
And the result?
You've guessed it:
   a sorry, mangled pulp –
   not just the shell broken
   but the kernel as well –
   utterly and hopelessly crushed.

It doesn't matter with nuts, Lord,
   but it does with people,
   for beneath a tough exterior
   most are fragile underneath.
Yet too often I'm clumsy in my dealings,
   coming down forcefully on little things
   when a quiet word would suffice,
   hopelessly heavy-handed
   when a light touch is all that's needed.
Teach me, Lord,
   if I would foster rather than shatter the spirit,
   to think fairly,
   love deeply
   and deal gently in all I do.
Amen.

58
The paint palette

It was a stunning selection:
  not just your run-of-the-mill colours
  but every shade in between –
  a diverse array of reds, yellows, blues, greens
  and innumerable others besides,
  enough to paint almost any scene
  and capture every nuance –
  an artist's delight.

Yet for all its breadth, Lord,
  that palette is as nothing compared to the one
  you have used in creation,
  its range of colours being magnified there
  a million times over:
  in the splendour of a sunset and magic of a rainbow,
  the hues of the sea and glory of the sky,
  the tints of autumn and tapestry of a garden,
  the plumage of birds and loveliness of a meadow.
An immeasurable spectrum brightens every day,
  causing me to catch my breath in wonder
  and exult in spirit.
For the imprint of your hand on the canvas of life,
  breathtaking beyond words,
  receive my praise.
Amen.

59
The feather

It fell from the sky,
    fluttering gently on the breeze,
    before landing in the palm of my hand
    with a touch so soft it barely registered.
Yet that same feather had helped carry a bird in flight,
    bearing its weight as wings strained against the wind,
    deceptive strength behind such apparent fragility.

Grant me, Lord, a similar combination:
    strength of faith, character, wisdom and purpose
    coupled with a gentleness of spirit;
    an inner steel
    matched by tenderness and humility
    in my dealings with others.
Though I am weak,
    may I be strong in you.
Amen.

60
The obstacle course

It was a challenge, no doubt about that –
    walls to scale,
    water to cross,
    ropes to climb,
    tunnels to negotiate –
    but, gruelling though it was
    and exhausted though they often felt,
    they stuck at it,
    tenaciously surmounting every obstacle
    in their resolve to complete the course.

Teach me, Lord, to persevere,
    not discouraged by the obstacles I meet along the way
    but recognising them as integral to the course,
    each a new challenge, to be faced with you.
However stiff the test or depleted my reserves,
    help me to battle on
    and run my race to the very end.
Amen.

61

The sunburn

I should have covered up,
    or splashed on the sun cream,
    but I didn't
    and paid the price,
    that extra half-hour in the sun a half-hour too much,
    turning a healthy tan into an ugly burn,
    a moment's pleasure into a week of pain.

So much in life, Lord, is special
    when enjoyed in moderation,
    but I indulge to excess,
    time and again craving that little bit more,
    rarely content with what I have.
Remind me
    that we can all have too much of a good thing,
    and help me to recognise when enough is enough.
Amen.

62
The label

I assumed it would be good,
   the best of its kind,
   for it was a familiar label,
   synonymous, to my mind, with quality.
But I was wrong,
   for the product was poor,
   the workmanship shoddy –
   not a patch on models half the price
   though less well known.

Teach me, Lord, to look behind the labels,
   especially when it comes to people,
   recognising that the terms so often used –
   East, West,
   black, white,
   Christian, Muslim,
   liberal, extremist –
   can only tell part of the story,
   never the whole.
Help me, in all my dealings with others,
   to see the person first
   and the label second.
Amen.

63
The motel

It wasn't the place for a holiday,
    still less where I'd choose to live,
    but it was clean, comfortable and convenient,
    ideal for a traveller looking to break his journey.

Remind me, Lord,
    that in this world I'm merely passing through;
    that, for all its beauty and wonder –
    the countless joys it has to offer –
    it's not my final destination
    but a staging post along the way.
Teach me, then, to celebrate everything it has to offer,
    yet not to be bound by it,
    to savour its many riches,
    but never to confuse them with blessings still to come.
Amen.

64
The maggots

They made my flesh crawl –
    a seething and wriggling multitude –
    yet they play their part in the intricate web of life,
    integral to the delicate balance of decay and renewal,
    new life emerging from old.

In the ugliness of death, Lord,
    speak of life born again,
    and in the apparent finality of the grave
    point to new beginnings.
Teach me that the close of one chapter
    is the opening of another,
    this world the gateway to your eternal kingdom.
Amen.

65
The breakdown lorry

It was a common enough sight,
    a breakdown van parked on the hard shoulder,
    lights flashing as its driver walked across
    to the stricken vehicle,
    but at that moment few sights were more welcome,
    for the vehicle was *ours*
    and we'd been waiting for what seemed an eternity
    for help to arrive.
No need to wait longer, though:
    a tweak here and twiddle there,
    and the job was done,
    the car fit again for us to complete our journey.

If only human hearts could be fixed so easily, Lord,
    how special that would be,
    but when lives are wrecked by sickness, fear,
    hurt and sorrow,
    they can break down completely,
    the business of repair a much longer process.
Reach out to all who feel they cannot carry on,
    and give them strength not just to resume their journey
    but to embark on it with confidence renewed
    and anticipation restored,
    able to see it safely through until they reach the end.
Amen.

66
The hosepipe ban

There was no crisis as yet,
  no cause for alarm,
  but reservoirs were low,
  the drought starting to bite
  and, with no rain forecast,
  stocks had to be used with care.
Yet when the ban was announced, folk were up in arms,
  baying for blood . . .
  for they couldn't hose their gardens or wash their cars!

I think, Lord, of the millions in this world
  who would gladly swap places –
  those for whom *any* water is a luxury.
I think of dehydrated children, dying of thirst,
  of communities whose supplies
  are polluted and diseased,
  of lands parched,
  pasture turned to dust.
And I'm ashamed,
  for like so many I'm swift to bemoan my lot
  and slow to count my blessings.
Teach me to understand how lucky I am
  and to think, for a change, of others instead of myself.
Amen.

67
The whitewash

It was basic, true,
    plain to the point of stark,
    but it did the job,
    covering a multitude of sins –
    cracks, hollows, stains and mould all neatly hidden –
    but, of course, it was no real answer,
    the problems merely masked rather than tackled,
    and it would be only a matter of time
    before they surfaced again,
    as bad as they were before.

There are as many faults in my life, Lord,
    and I try the same trick,
    attempting to whitewash over them,
    hide them from view.
But only *you* can do that,
    your love covering what I can never hope to conceal.
Come now,
    and though my sins are as scarlet,
    make me whiter than snow.
Amen.

68
The bird cage

It was a decent size and well equipped,
   not your average bird cage,
   but it was a cage nonetheless,
   its purpose to confine,
   hold captive,
   lest its occupant break free.

Our cages are hidden, Lord,
   but just as real,
   the bars of fear as impregnable as any prison,
   of insecurity as any cell,
   of prejudice as any jail,
   of self as any dungeon.
Unlock the door and break our bonds,
   that we might be truly free.
Amen.

69
The stopwatch

They were racing against the clock,
   every millisecond counting,
   so the athletes strained forward,
   limbs pumping,
   lungs bursting,
   determined to set a new fastest time.

The older I get, Lord, the more life feels like that,
   as though the stopwatch is running
   and time is running *out*,
   so I rush around from one thing to the next
   determined to cram ever more
   into the unforgiving minute.
Yet so easily, in my haste, I forget to enjoy what I have,
   to let go of striving and simply to live.
Remind me
   that though this mortal span may be slipping away,
   it is just a taste of things to come;
   that though the days are passing,
   I have no cause to fret,
   for with you I have all the time in the world . . .
   and far, far beyond!
Amen.

70
The patch of grass

It was nothing special,
   just an ordinary patch of grass,
   no different from the meadow in which they stood,
   yet the cows were straining to nibble it,
   heads thrusting eagerly through the fence
   as though there were no tomorrow
   and this was the choicest of feasts.

I laughed, Lord,
   but I shouldn't have,
   for though I know it's foolish,
   I too assume the grass is greener on the other side,
   time after time coveting what I do not have
   and hankering after what I cannot reach,
   as though I'm somehow missing out
   on what others around me enjoy.
Teach me, instead, to count my blessings,
   more than I can number,
   and to be content.
Amen.

71
The balloon

She skipped along,
    holding it high,
    proud of her new balloon,
    her mind full of the games she would play with it
    and the fun it would bring –
    delights she would long enjoy.
But then:
    a tree,
    a thorn,
    a bang . . .
    and all her dreams were gone.

My happiness, Lord, seems more secure,
    more solid,
    but it's not,
    for it too is so easily punctured,
    few things as permanent as they seem.
Teach me to trust in you,
    knowing that though all else may fail,
    you will not.
Amen.

72
The berries

They looked good,
   succulent and tasty,
   and for the birds, at least, they were just that,
   a welcome meal through the lean months of winter.
But, of course, appearances deceived,
   any meal *I* made of them likely to be my last.

Teach me, Lord, not to be taken in
   by what looks appealing
   but finally destroys,
   what promises satisfaction
   yet ultimately poisons within.
However enticing temptation may be,
   help me to see where it might lead
   and to avoid its hidden dangers.
Amen.

73

The fallen tree

It was hard to believe –
    the mighty tree that had stood for so long,
    felled by the gale –
    yet the proof was there before me,
    the roots laid bare,
    trunk prostrate,
    branches smashed and splintered.
Its strength had been its undoing,
    for, unable to bend,
    it had caught the full force of the wind
    and been sent crashing to the ground.

Teach me, Lord, that though at times I need to stand firm,
    unyielding on matters of faith and principle,
    at other times I must be ready to give a little,
    recognising my limitations,
    open to new insights
    and bowing to the wisdom of others.
Help me to know which time is which,
    and give me, as appropriate,
    the courage or humility to do both.
Amen.

74
The kitchen scales

Six ounces of sugar,
   six of flour,
   six more of margarine –
   carefully I weighed out the ingredients,
   resolved to get them right.
Too little of one,
   too much of another,
   and the balance would be skewed,
   the cake spoiled,
   my efforts a waste of time.

Teach me, Lord, to weigh up my life,
   assessing what goes into it
   and what comes out;
   to make time for work and rest,
   reflection and action,
   myself and others,
   this world and your kingdom.
Teach me to find a place for all,
   keeping each in balance with the rest,
   so that, from the ingredients you've given,
   I may make the most of life,
   now and for all eternity.
Amen.

75

The ream of paper

It was a mess,
    the page a mass of corrections,
    not just one or two
    but hundreds,
    and the result was a shambles.
Yet no matter,
    for I'd a *ream* of paper to work with –
    not just one clean sheet,
    but another . . .
    and another . . .
    and another . . .
    as many, surely, as I could ever want.

Thank you, Lord, for the clean sheet *you* offer
    when I make a mess of life;
    your invitation to turn over a new leaf and start again.
Thank you that your mercy is never exhausted,
    your patience never at an end;
    that you go on offering new beginnings
    for as many times as it takes.
Amen.

76
The all-weather sports pitch

The wind blew and heavens opened,
   but though all around rain stopped play,
   they carried on with their game,
   for the pitch was built to withstand the elements,
   summer or winter,
   day or night –
   ready, in all weathers,
   like the players themselves,
   for play to continue.

Forgive me, Lord,
   for though I speak of commitment,
   mine's a fair-weather discipleship,
   strong enough when the sun shines,
   but swift to founder should the wind blow cold.
Give me a faith for all seasons,
   as true to you in calm or storm
   as you are true to me.
Amen.

77
The hand of cards

I wanted to follow suit
    but I couldn't,
    for my hand was bare of the suit in question,
    so I had to discard,
    watching helplessly while others took the tricks.

I don't mind that in cards, Lord,
    for it's only a game,
    but when it comes to serving you it's different,
    for you have shown me in Christ
    the way I ought to live,
    and there too I yearn to follow suit.
But though the spirit's willing,
    the flesh is weak,
    the commitment I profess found wanting
    when the chips are down.
Forgive all that's lacking within me,
    and what I cannot do *alone*,
    help me to do with *you*.
Amen.

78
The flower arrangers

They'd been there all day,
    painstakingly cutting, wiring, arranging and adjusting,
    each weaving an intricate floral tapestry,
    a glorious fusion of scent and colour.
They hadn't made the *blooms*, of course,
    the beauty of those being down to another creator,
    but they'd helped to fashion what he'd provided,
    aligning their gifts with his.

Help me likewise, Lord,
    to work *with* rather than *against* you –
    to live in tune with your creation,
    in harmony with your will
    and in partnership with others.
Instead of squandering your countless gifts
    or taking your blessings for granted,
    teach me to consecrate every aspect of life
    to your service,
    and to create from it all something beautiful for you.
Amen.

79
The twilight

The light was fading but not yet gone,
    suffusing the air with a kind of magic
    as life everywhere readied itself for slumber –
    the bustle of the morning long past
    and heat of the day forgotten
    as the chill of night descended,
    precursor to another day.

It set me thinking, Lord, of those in their twilight years,
    the sun beginning to set yet not quite faded.
Though the energy of youth is long past
    and aspirations of middle years seem distant,
    may this time of life bring joys of its own:
    an inner tranquillity and contentment
    in light of all that has gone before,
    coupled with confident trust in what is yet to come –
    the new dawn that, by your grace,
    will surely follow the night.
Amen.

80
The soup

We murmured appreciatively,
   licking our lips in anticipation,
   for the soup smelt good,
   a perfect way to start the meal.
And though it was soon finished,
   our bowls pushed aside,
   no matter,
   for it was just the first course –
   plenty more to come.

Only suddenly, Lord,
   I thought of the vagrant queuing at the hostel,
   his ladle of soup not a starter
   but the only meal he'd eat that day;
   nothing fine or fancy about it,
   yet to him a feast,
   bringing a little succour to his ravaged body,
   a respite from the winter's chill . . .
   and I could eat no more,
   my meal having lost its savour.
Teach me, Lord, in my plenty,
   to remember those with so much less,
   for should I forget them,
   I forget you too.
Amen.

81
The failed exam

Could I have passed?
It's hard to say.
I like to think so,
 but the exam was tough,
 and the subject not one that came naturally to me.
But I'd worked at it,
 given my all,
 so though the result was disappointing,
 at least I'd tried.

Lord, when it comes to serving you,
 you don't expect perfection,
 my life, under your examination,
 invariably falling short.
What you do ask
 is that I genuinely try to walk the way of Christ.
Though I go on getting it wrong day after day,
 rarely even approaching the sort of standard I'd like,
 teach me never to lose heart
 or to stop striving to serve you better,
 for your love is as much for those
 who've tried and failed
 as for anyone else –
 perhaps for those most of all.
 Amen.

82
The feather duster

I rarely used it,
    but I should have done,
    for when I stopped to look
    there were cobwebs everywhere,
    trailing from the walls and ceiling in room after room,
    each a sign of complacency,
    of a spring-clean long overdue.

My faith, Lord, is cloaked with cobwebs,
    having been left untouched too often and too long,
    neglected to the point of being redundant.
I've been complacent,
    assuming discipleship can look after itself
    instead of needing a regular dusting down.
Forgive me,
    and may your Spirit sweep through my life,
    freshening up my faith
    and breathing new life within.
Amen.

83
The headache tablet

It was nothing major,
    more of a dull ache than a pain,
    but I felt sorry for myself nonetheless,
    enough to reach for the headache tablets,
    and mope around miserably
    until the last trace of discomfort had gone.

Forgive me, Lord,
    for I forget those who live in constant pain,
    longing for release yet finding no end to their suffering,
    each day blighted by its stranglehold.
Give them strength not just to get through
    but also to find joy and fulfilment in life,
    and grant the assurance that,
    just as you shared our sufferings in Christ,
    so, through him,
    we will all finally enter a brighter kingdom
    in which pain and sorrow will be at an end.
Amen.

84
The returned goods

There was a counter set aside,
    dealing solely with faulty items;
    and a crowd stood there,
    queuing to return their goods
    and claim a refund.
They had no need to argue
    for it was taken as read:
    the product was substandard,
    unacceptable to all.

You could reject *me* just as easily, Lord,
    replace me for another model with equal grounds,
    for I fall short in so many ways
    of the person I ought to be.
Yet, for all my faults, you refuse to let me go,
    counting me of inestimable value,
    and working tirelessly to make me new.
For that patient and faithful love,
    thank you.
Amen.

85
The photocopier

It ran off the copies in no time,
    each of them perfect,
    an exact replica of the one before –
    so simple yet so effective –
    achieving in minutes
    what it would have taken me hours to do by hand.

Lord, you do not expect me to be just like you,
    and you do not want all your people to be clones,
    each thinking and acting the same,
    but you *do* want something of Christ to show
    in the lives of those who follow you.
Work within me,
    so that, despite all that mars the picture,
    at least a little of his love, joy and goodness
    may shine through.
Amen.

86
The oil slick

It wasn't quite the disaster of old,
    for advances had been made,
    technology yielding ways to contain the spill
    and limit the damage,
    but the oil was there nonetheless:
    choking, killing, soiling, polluting,
    leaving a stain on all it touched –
    so swift to form,
    so hard to remove.

Our world is stained, Lord,
    engulfed by a black tide of injustice, intolerance,
    fear and hatred
    that desecrates and destroys countless lives
    and, for all our so-called advances,
    we're no nearer containing it than we've ever been.
Come to our aid,
    and cleanse us of all that denies and divides –
    that precludes joy and crushes hope.
Transform what we can never change ourselves,
    and make all things new.
Amen.

87
The wet soap

I grabbed it
   and grabbed it again,
   like a novice juggler learning his trade,
   but the soap was wet
   and it fell from my grasp,
   too slippery to hold.

So much in life is the same, Lord:
   impossible to hold on to.
I think it's mine,
   safely secured,
   only for it to slip away –
   here one minute and gone the next.
Teach me to celebrate the joys of this world
   but to root my happiness in what lies beyond it –
   in your love that never ends
   and that nothing can take away.
Amen.

88
The Internet chat room

They chatted together,
 an astonishing assortment of different ages,
 cultures, creeds and backgrounds;
 in so many ways, miles apart,
 yet, thanks to modern technology, brought close,
 as though they were there together in the one room.

Overcome, Lord, the barriers that keep us apart,
 dividing person from person
 and race from race –
 East and West,
 black and white,
 male and female,
 rich and poor.
Whatever our colour, culture or creed,
 draw us together and heal our wounds –
 so that we may live and work together as one people,
 one world.
Amen.

89
The tennis court

The lines were clearly marked,
    each of them integral to the court,
    indicating whether the ball was long or short,
    in or out.
They set the boundaries,
    the confines of the game,
    everything plain to all.

Lord, you set boundaries for *me*,
    not to restrict or confine
    but to give definition to who and what I am –
    your love the space in which I live,
    your guidance giving parameters to my life
    and your mercy placing me back within them
    when I step over the line.
For the meaning and direction I find in you,
    receive my praise.
Amen.

90
The sparrow

I caught the movement as I crouched in the hide –
   a sudden flutter of wings –
   and, grabbing my binoculars, I scanned the trees,
   excited,
   expectant,
   straining to catch a sight . . .
   but then
   disappointment
   and dismay
   for it was nothing interesting,
   nothing rare . . .
   only a sparrow.

Only a sparrow?
What do I mean, Lord?
It may be plain,
   but, like everything else in the world,
   it's a miracle,
   a wonder,
   special beyond words –
   each bone and feather a work of art,
   fashioned by your hands and speaking of you.
However ordinary it may seem or familiar it may be,
   teach me never to lose my sense of wonder
   at all you have made.
Amen.

91

The investment

I cashed the policy,
    frustrated by the lack of growth,
    then invested it again,
    seeking a better return,
    a higher yield for my cash.
And it seemed a shrewd move,
    for it swiftly grew,
    exceeding all expectations –
    a tidy nest egg for the years ahead.
Yet through whose hands did it pass to do so?
What activities did it finance,
    exploitation collude in
    and dubious dealings tacitly approve?

Lord, I mean no harm to anyone,
    my aim simply to put a little bit aside,
    but save me, in investing my money,
    from inadvertently selling my soul.
Amen.

92
The apology

She didn't find it easy, I could see that,
   words not just hard to find
   but harder still to say.
Yet she'd done wrong
   and was truly sorry,
   had made a mistake
   and wanted to make amends,
   the apology, if not the most gracious,
   nonetheless sincere,
   straight from the heart.

I've no problem saying sorry to *you*, Lord –
   I do it all the time –
   but unless my apologies are real,
   backed up by genuine remorse
   and a true desire to change,
   they mean nothing –
   all just empty words.
Teach me not just to *say* sorry
   but to mean it.
Amen.

93
The weever fish

One minute he was paddling happily,
    laughing as he splashed in the waves,
    but the next he cried out in pain
    and ran screaming to his mother amidst floods of tears.
A weever fish had stung him,
    not with any malice but out of self-defence,
    instinctively releasing its poison
    as the boy's foot came near –
    with agonising results.

Teach me, Lord, that the hurt people cause
    is not always intended,
    so much of what they say and do
    an instinctive response
    rather than premeditated.
Help me, then,
    when my instinct is to lash out and hurt in turn,
    to bear the wounds with grace,
    remembering how you so willingly
    were wounded for all in Christ.
Amen.

94
The remote control

I flicked through channels,
   scrolled through text,
   recorded programmes,
   switched on and off,
   everything controlled at the touch of a button –
   volume, brightness, colour, contrast adjusted with ease,
   without even moving from my chair.

Can't you, Lord, control this world you've made,
   putting an end to its hatred, sorrow, pain and death?
Can't you turn war to peace,
   evil to good,
   sickness to health
   and darkness to light,
   all at the touch of your hand?
But that's the wrong question, isn't it,
   for you *can* and *do* change things,
   only not remotely but by consent,
   not *controlling* what we do
   but *inviting* our response.
And though the price can be high,
   I wouldn't have it any other way,
   for I'd much rather be a person than a puppet.
Thank you, Lord, for freedom to choose,
   and teach me to use it wisely.
Amen.

95
The chess game

I spotted the mistake almost immediately
    but it was too late to do anything about it,
    for the move was made
    and the damage done.
There could be no turning the clock back and trying again,
    no second chance or court of appeal.
I'd blundered
    and had to face the consequences,
    salvaging the situation as best I could.

So easily, Lord, I act in haste
    and live to regret it,
    errors of judgement
    having repercussions I never considered,
    affecting not just me but others too.
And, much though I wish it was otherwise,
    I can't put the clock back,
    undoing what's been done.
Yet *you*, Lord, *do* give a second chance,
    ready to put my mistakes behind me,
    as though they have never been.
Teach me, in all I do, to think first,
    considering where it might lead
    and, when I get things wrong,
    as I so often do,
    forgive me
    and help me to start again.
Amen.

96

The frayed rope

It had been strong once,
   easily able to bear the load and take the strain,
   but the rope now was frayed –
   just about serviceable,
   but *only* just:
   the question not *if* it would snap
   but *when*.

It reminded me, Lord, of people,
   so many worn to breaking point,
   ground down by sickness, hurt, worry and fear,
   by the ravages of time,
   and uncertain how much longer they can cope.
Reach out to strengthen and restore,
   from the tangled threads of their lives
   weaving cords that will not be broken.
Amen.

97
The cross-country run

I was exhausted at the end,
    feet sore,
    legs like jelly,
    the heavy ground having taken its toll.
And as for the next day –
    well, let's just put it like this:
    I knew I'd been in a race!

I talk of discipleship in such terms, Lord –
    as a stiff test,
    demanding examination,
    calling for perseverance if I'm to finish the course –
    but does the practice match the theory,
    does commitment, in reality, ask anything of me at all?
Forgive me,
    for my words say one thing but my deeds another,
    the faith I settle for
    rarely making demands on the way I live,
    still less taking as much out of me as it puts in.
Teach me truly to follow,
    truly to serve,
    so that I may not just *talk* of discipleship
    but know I've run the race.
Amen.

98
The molehill

It looked a mess,
    the lawn ruined by a single mole,
    months of raking, mowing, feeding and weeding
    undermined overnight.
But the damage was superficial
    and easily enough put right –
    in a few weeks rectified as though it had never been.

There are molehills in my life, Lord –
    problems, trials and disagreements
    that get under my skin –
    but most of them are minor rather than major,
    a nuisance,
    nothing more.
Forgive me for turning them into mountains,
    magnifying them out of all proportion
    until I can see nothing else.
Give me, in all things, a proper sense of perspective,
    lest the biggest problem I face is *me*.
Amen.

99
The shopping trolley

She couldn't have managed without it,
    the weight of shopping simply too much
    for a woman of her years,
    but the trolley she pulled solved the problem,
    bearing a load she could never have carried alone –
    an impossible burden suddenly made light.

Thank you, Lord, that when I wrestle with heavy loads,
    weighed down by problems that sap my strength
    and troubles that crush the spirit,
    you unfailingly come to my aid,
    helping to shoulder
    what I can no longer manage to bear.
Thank you for being there when I need you most,
    ready to carry not only the burden
    but me as well.
Amen.

100
The canal boat

I'd have been faster walking,
   our progress leisurely to say the least,
   but in that lay its charm:
   this a trip to be savoured,
   celebrated,
   taking in the sights and sounds along the way –
   the journey as much a pleasure as the destination.

Teach me, Lord,
   though my destination lies beyond this world,
   to celebrate the journey of *life*,
   recognising the innumerable ways
   it can fill me with joy,
   touch me with wonder
   and move me to gratitude.
Save me from being so full of heaven
   that I lose sight of earth,
   from dwelling so much on joys to come
   that I close my eyes to blessings now.
You offer life in all its fullness.
Teach me to live it now.
Amen.